CW00541273

**THE ROYAL COURT THEATRE
PRESENTS**

Human Animals

by Stef Smith

Human Animals is part of the Royal Court's
Jerwood New Playwrights Programme, supported by
the Jerwood Charitable Foundation.

Human Animals was first performed at the Royal
Court Jerwood Theatre Upstairs, Sloane Square, on
Wednesday 18th May 2016.

Human Animals
by Stef Smith

CAST (in alphabetical order)

Alex **Natalie Dew**
John **Ian Gelder**
Nancy **Stella Gonet**
Lisa **Lisa McGrillis**
Si **Sargon Yelda**
Jamie **Ashley Zhangazha**

Director **Hamish Pirie**
Designer **Camilla Clarke**
Lighting Designer **Lizzie Powell**
Composer & Sound Designer **Mark Melville**
Movement Director **Frauke Requardt**
Casting Director **Amy Ball**
Assistant Director **Sian Davila**
Production Manager **Matt Noddings**
Fight Director **Bret Yount**
Costume Supervisor **Natasha Ward**
Stage Managers **Jason Mills, Kate Wilson**
Stage Management Work Placement **Sayeedah Supersad**
Set Construction by **Form and Function**

The Royal Court & Stage Management wish to thank the following for their help on this production:
Ricky Keane - Supreme Animal Foods, Lewisham

Human Animals
by Stef Smith

Stef Smith (Writer)

Theatre includes: **Swallow (Traverse); Remote (NT Connections); And The Beat Goes On (Random Accomplice/Horsecross); Cured (The Arches, Glasgow); Woman of the Year (Òran Mór); Grey Matter (Lemon Tree, Aberdeen); Falling/Flying (Tron); Roadkill (Edinburgh Festival Fringe).**

Awards include: **Olivier Award for Outstanding Achievement in an Affiliate Theatre, Critics Award for Theatre in Scotland for Best New Production, Amnesty International Expression of Freedom Award, Herald Angel Award, Total Theatre Award for Innovation, The Scotsman Fringe First Award (Roadkill); Scottish Arts Club Theatre Award for Drama, The Scotsman Fringe First Award (Swallow).**

Stef has been awarded the New Playwright Award by Playwrights Studio, Scotland. Stef was a member of the Royal Court National Writers Group in 2013. She is an Associate Artist at the Traverse Theatre.

Camilla Clarke (Designer)

Other theatre includes: **Yuri (Chapter, Cardiff); Triptych (De Oscuro); Seagulls (Volcano); The Wonderful Wold of Dissocia (RWCMD).**

As Assistant Designer: **Candy Lion, Mother Courage, Mametz (National Theatre Wales).**

Awards include: **Linbury Prize for Stage Design.**

Sian Davila (Assistant Director)

As Director, theatre includes: **London Eyes (Belarus Free Theatre/Young Vic); Collected Stories (Stonecrabs/Albany).**

As Assistant Director, theatre includes: **We'll Always Have Paris (South London Theatre); ASK (Islington Community Theatre).**

As Co-producer, theatre includes: **Labyrinth (Almeida).**

Natalie Dew (Alex)

For the Royal Court: **Teh Internet Is Serious Business, Rough Cuts.**

Other theatre includes: **Bend It Like Beckham (West End); Twelfth Night (Liverpool Everyman); Fault Lines (Hampstead Theatre); Romeo & Juliet (National); Arab Nights (Metta); Hamlet (Northern Broadsides); Arabian Nights (RSC); As You Like It (Dash Arts); Hansel & Gretel (Catherine Wheels); Twelfth Night (New Shakespeare).**

Television includes: **Lewis, Gavin & Stacey.**

Ian Gelder (John)

For the Royal Court: **The Low Road, Fireface, Mouth to Mouth (& West End).**

Other theatre includes: **Gods & Monsters (Southwark); Titus Andronicus (Globe); Roots, Good, The Front Page (Donmar); King Lear (Almeida); Definitely the Bahamas (Orange Tree); Company, Racing Demon (Crucible, Sheffield); Precious Little Talent (Trafalgar Studios); Lingua Franca (Finborough/ Broadway); Serious Money, Divine Right (Birmingham Rep); The Sound of Music (West End); The Crucible (& West End), The Merchant of Venice (& World Tour), The Taming of the Shrew, Richard III, Titus Andronicus (RSC); Henry IV Parts 1 & 2, His Dark Materials, Stuff Happens, The Power of Yes (National); A Passage to India, Anna Karenina, Heartbreak House (Shared Experience); Three Sisters (Chichester Festival); Martin Yesterday (Royal Exchange, Manchester); Poor Superman (& Traverse), Apocalyptica (Hampstead); Mrs Warren's Profession (Lyric Hammersmith); Two Lips Indifferent Red (Bush); Richard II (Bristol Old Vic).**

Television includes: **EastEnders, Ripper Street, Game of Thrones, Mr Selfridge, Endeavour, Psychoville, Silent Witness, Torchwood, Robin Hood, Fallen Angel, Casualty, The Bill, Absolutely Fabulous, Blackeyes, The Day Today.**

Film includes: **Little Dorrit, The Fool, King Ralph.**

Stella Gonet (Nancy)

For the Royal Court: **Hope, Slab Boy Trilogy (& Traverse).**

Theatre includes: **A Further Education, Hilda (Hampstead); For Services Rendered (Chichester Festival); Handbagged (& West End), Women, Power & Politics (Tricycle); Before the Party (Almeida); Top Girls (Out of Joint/Chichester/Trafalgar Studios); Skylight (& National), The Memory Of Water (West End); Measure for Measure, After Easter, A Midsummer Night's Dream, Divine Gossip, Three Sisters, The Revenger's Tragedy, The Jew of Malta, Fashion, Heresies, The Archbishop's Ceiling (RSC); Racing Demon, The Shaughraun, The Voysey Inheritance, Hamlet, True Dare Kiss, Command or Promise (National); Cyrano De Bergerac (Theatre Royal Haymarket).**

Television includes: **Humans, Father Brown, Hacks, Lewis, Mo, Holby City, Rebus, Roman Mysteries, Persuasion, Dalziel & Pascoe, Mysterious Murders, Where the Heart Is, Murder in Suburbia, Taggart, The Inspector Lynley Mysteries, Foyle's War, Midsomer Murders, The Secret, Verdict, Supply & Demand, The Crow Road, Trip Trap, The House of Eliott, The Advocates, The Common Pursuit, Heading**

Home, The Bill, Down Where The Buffalo Go, Casualty, The Shutter Falls, To Have & to Hold.

Film includes: **Just Gone, How I Live Now, Dirty Bomb, Nicholas Nickleby, Stalin, For Queen & Country.**

Lisa McGrillis (Lisa)

For the Royal Court: **The Pass.**

Other theatre includes: **Much Ado About Nothing, The Globe Mysteries (Globe); The Pitmen Painters (& Broadway/National), A Sock in the Wash, Nicole (Live); The Awkward Squad (West End); Hansel & Gretel, Tattercoats (Northern Stage); Tonic (Open Clasp).**

Television includes: **Mum, The Musketeers, Fungus the Bogey Man, George Gently, Hebburn, Rocket Man, Spit Game.**

Film includes: **The Pass, Much Ado About Nothing, The Other Possibility.**

Mark Melville (Composer & Sound Designer)

For the Royal Court: **Violence & Son, God Bless the Child.**

Other theatre includes: **The Destroyed Room (Vanishing Point/BAC); Wit (Royal Exchange, Manchester); Yer Granny, Knives in Hens, Miracle Man, Empty, My Shrinking Life (National Theatre of Scotland); Tomorrow (Vanishing Point/Cena Contemporânea Festival, Brasil/ Brighton Festival/Tramway/National); Dragon (Vox Motus/National Theatre of Scotland/ Tianjin People's Art Theatre, China); The Beautiful Cosmos of Ivor Cutler (Vanishing Point/National Theatre of Scotland); Swallows & Amazons, Grimm Tales (Theatre by the Lake, Keswick); Saturday Night (Vanishing Point/ National Theatre of Portugal); Pride & Prejudice (Two Bit Classics); Mister Holgado (Unicorn); A Midsummer Night's Dream (Royal Lyceum, Edinburgh); Wonderland (Vanishing Point/Napoli Teatro Festival Italia/Tramway/Edinburgh International Festival); Mwana (Ankur/Tron); The Beggar's Opera (Vanishing Point/Royal Lyceum, Edinburgh/Belgrade, Coventry); What Happened Was This, One Night Stand, Naked Neighbour Twitching Blind (Never Did Nothing/ Tron/Tramway); The Crucible, A Tender Thing, Hamlet, Your Country Needs You (but I don't need my country), Pierrepoint, The Unsociables, The BFG, Two, Merlin, Quicksand, The Snow Queen, Peter Pan, Children of Killers, Of Mice & Men, Jason & the Argonauts, The Crucible (The Dukes, Lancaster).**

Dance includes: **In a Deep Dark Wood (Gobbledegook/Moko Dance); Best Friends (M6/ Ludus).**

Awards include: **Critics Award for Theatre in Scotland for Best Technical Presentation (Dragon); Critics Award for Theatre in Scotland for Best Music & Sound (The Beautiful Cosmos of Ivor Cutler); UK Theatre Award for Best Show for Children & Young People (Mister Holgado).**

Mark is an Associate Artist of The Dukes,

Lancaster and is also currently developing a new theatre and ideas company with director, Louie Ingham. In April, they launched Point to Point, an audio theatre experience as part of the Lakes Ignite 2015 Festival.

Hamish Pirie (Director)

For the Royal Court: **Violence & Son, Who Cares, Teh Internet is Serious Business.**

Other theatre includes: **Shibboleth (Abbey, Dublin); I'm With The Band (Traverse/Wales Millennium Centre); Quiz Show, Demos, 50 Plays for Edinburgh (Traverse); Love With A Capital 'L', 3 Seconds, Most Favoured, The Last Bloom (Traverse/Òran Mór); Bravo Figaro (Royal Opera House/Traverse); Salt Root & Roe (Donmar/ Trafalgar); Stacy (& Trafalgar), Purgatory (Arcola); Pennies (nabokov); Paper House (Flight 5065).**

Hamish trained as Resident Assistant Director at Paines Plough & at the Donmar Warehouse. He was previously Associate Director at the Traverse Theatre. Hamish is an Associate Director at the Royal Court.

Lizzie Powell (Lighting Designer)

For the Royal Court: **Violence & Son.**

Other theatre includes: **Endgame, The Choir, Fever Dream: Southside, The Libertine, Far Away/Seagulls, Krapp's Last Tape/ Footfalls (Citizens); The Brink (Orange Tree); Fruit Trilogy (West Yorkshire Playhouse); Romeo and Juliet (Crucible, Sheffield); Anna Karenina (Royal Exchange, Manchester/West Yorkshire Playhouse); Secret Theatre (Lyric, Hammersmith/Tour); Our Ladies of Perpetual Succour, In A Time O' Strife, Glasgow Girls, My Shrinking Life, The Enquirer, An Appointment with the Wickerman, Knives in Hens, Girl X, Transform: Glasgow, Mary Queen of Scots Got Her Head Chopped Off, Our Teacher's a Troll, Rupture, Venus as a Boy (National Theatre of Scotland); White Gold (Iron Oxide); Idomeneus (Gate); Cinderella, Mother Goose, Jack & the Beanstalk (Perth); Caged, Poppy & Dingan, The Book of Beasts (Catherine Wheels); Spring Awakening, While You Lie, Any Given Day, The Dark Things (Traverse); Pangaa (Ankur); Huxley's Lab (Grid Iron/Lung Ha's/Edinburgh Festival Theatre); Under Milk Wood (Theatre Royal, Northampton); The Death of Harry Leon, Making History (Ouroboros); Cockroach, The Dogstone/Nasty, Brutish & Short, Nobody Will Ever Forgive Us (National Theatre of Scotland/ Traverse).**

Frauke Requardt (Movement Director)

Dance includes: **The Roof (National/Fuel/LIFT/ Requardt&Rosenberg); Motorshow (LIFT/ Without Walls/Requardt&Rosenberg); Electric Hotel (Fuel/Without Walls/ Requardt&Rosenberg); What We Love (Richmond Library); Episode (& Tour), Jammy Dodgers (& Tour), Roadkill Café (The Place); Pequeñas Delicías (Bogota, Columbia); Pictures from an**

Exhibition (Young Vic/Sadler's Wells).

Awards include: **Capture5 Award (Still Moving).**

Frauke is a Director and Choreographer, working in theatre amongst other art forms. She largely creates her own dance works, and she formerly performed with Lea Anderson's Cholmondeleys. She has an ongoing collaboration with theatre maker David Rosenberg. As Requardt&Rosenberg, they create large-scale outdoor dance works. Her work often contains live music. She is an Associate Artist at both The Place and Greenwich Dance, and is currently writing her Masters dissertation in Existential Psychotherapy.

Sargon Yelda (Si)

For the Royal Court: **Teh Internet is Serious Business.**

Other theatre includes: **Forget Me Not, Incognito (Bush/HighTide); Light Shining in Buckinghamshire, Dara, Emperor & Galilean, Mother Courage & Her Children (National); Moby Dick, The Cabinet of Dr Caligari (Arcola/ Simple8); The Comedy of Errors, Twelfth Night, The Tempest (RSC); When the Rain Stops Falling (Almeida); Salt Meets Wound (503).**

Television includes: **Zen, Compulsion, Midnight Man, Saddam's Tribe.**

Film includes: **Spectre, Dead Cat.**

Radio includes: **Look Who's Back, The Afghan & the Penguin, The Casper Logue Affair.**

Ashley Zhangazha (Jamie)

For the Royal Court: **Belong, Truth & Reconciliation.**

Other theatre includes: **A Raisin in the Sun, Macbeth (Crucible, Sheffield); Image of an Unknown Young Woman (Gate); Ah, Wilderness! (Young Vic); Hamlet (Royal Exchange, Manchester); Venice Preserv'd (The Spectators Guild); Henry V, Oliver, Fences (& Theatre Royal, Bath), Whistle Down the Wind (West End); Richard II, King Lear (Donmar); Danton's Death (National).**

Television includes: **Humans, Ordinary Lies.**

Radio includes: **Rasselas - Prince of Abyssinia.**

Awards include: **1'st Prize Ian Charleson Award for Macbeth (Crucible, Sheffield).**

JERWOOD CHARITABLE FOUNDATION

Jerwood New Playwrights is a longstanding partnership between Jerwood Charitable Foundation and the Royal Court. Each year, Jerwood New Playwrights supports the production of three new works by emerging writers, all of whom are in the first 10 years of their career.

The Royal Court carefully identifies playwrights whose careers would benefit from the challenge and profile of being fully produced either in the Jerwood Downstairs or Jerwood Upstairs Theatres at the Royal Court.

Since 1994, the programme has produced a collection of challenging and outspoken works which explore a variety of new forms and voices and so far has supported the production of 81 new plays. These plays include: Joe Penhall's **Some Voices**, Nick Grosso's **Peaches** and **Real Classy Affair**, Judy Upton's **Ashes and Sand**, Sarah Kane's **Blasted, Cleansed** and **4.48 Psychosis**, Michael Wynne's **The Knocky** and **The People are Friendly**, Judith Johnson's **Uganda**, Sebastian Barry's **The Steward of Christendom**, Jez Butterworth's **Mojo**, Mark Ravenhill's **Shopping and Fucking**, Ayub Khan Din's **East is East** and **Notes on Falling Leaves**, Martin McDonagh's **The Beauty Queen of Leenane**, Jess Walters' **Cockroach, Who?**, Tamantha Hammerschlag's **Backpay**, Connor McPherson's **The Weir**, Meredith Oakes' **Faith**, Rebecca Prichard's **Fair Game**, Roy Williams' **Lift Off, Clubland** and **Fallout**, Richard Bean's **Toast** and **Under the Whaleback**, Gary Mitchell's **Trust** and **The Force of Change**, Mick Mahoney's **Sacred Heart** and **Food Chain**, Marina Carr's **On Raftery's Hill**, David Eldridge's **Under the Blue Sky** and **Incomplete and Random Acts of Kindness**, David Harrower's **Presence**, Simon Stephens' **Herons, Country Music**

and **Motortown**, Leo Butler's **Redundant** and **Lucky Dog**, Enda Walsh's **Bedbound**, David Greig's **Outlying Islands**, Zinnie Harris' **Nightingale and Chase**, Grae Cleugh's **Fucking Games**, Rona Munro's **Iron**, Ché Walker's **Fleshwound**, Laura Wade's **Breathing Corpses**, debbie tucker green's **Stoning Mary**, Gregory Burke's **On Tour**, Stella Feehily's **O Go My Man**, Simon Faquhar' **Rainbow Kiss**, April de Angelis, Stella Feehily, Tanika Gupta, Chloe Moss and Laura Wade's **Catch**, Polly Stenham's **That Face** and **Tusk Tusk**, Mike Bartlett's **My Child**, Fiona Evans' **Scarborough**, Levi David Addai's **Oxford Street**, Bola Agbaje's **Gone Too Far!** and **Off The Endz**, Alexi Kaye Campbell's **The Pride**, Alia Bano's **Shades**, Tim Crouch's **The Autho** DC Moore's **The Empire**, Anya Reiss' **Spur of the Moment** and **The Acid Test**, Penelope Skinner's **The Village Bike**, Rachel De-lahay's **The Westbridge** and **Routes**, Nick Payne's **Constellations**, Vivienne Franzmann's **The Witness** and **Pests**, E. V. Crowe's **Hero**, Anders Lustgarten's **If You Don't Let Us Dream, We Won't Let You Sleep**, Suhayla El-Bushra's **Pigeons**, Clare Lizzimore's **Mint**, Alistair McDowall's **Talk Show**, Rory Mullarkey **The Wolf From The Door**, Molly Davies' **God Bless The Child**, Diana Nneka Atuona's **Liberian Girl** and Cordelia Lynn's **Lela & Co**

Jerwood Charitable Foundation is dedicated to imaginative and responsible revenue funding of the arts, supporting artists to develop and grow at important stages in their careers. It works with artists across art forms, from dance and theatre to literature, music and the visual arts.

jerwoodcharitablefoundation.org

THE ROYAL COURT THEATRE

The Royal Court Theatre is the writers' theatre. It is the leading force in world theatre for energetically cultivating writers – undiscovered, emerging and established.

Through the writers, the Royal Court is at the forefront of creating restless, alert, provocative theatre about now. We open our doors to the unheard voices and free thinkers that, through their writing, change our way of seeing.

Over 120,000 people visit the Royal Court in Sloane Square, London, each year and many thousands more see our work elsewhere through transfers to the West End and New York, UK and international tours, digital platforms, our residencies across London, and our site-specific work. Through all our work we strive to inspire audiences and influence future writers with radical thinking and provocative discussion.

The Royal Court's extensive development activity encompasses a diverse range of writers and artists and includes an ongoing programme of writers' attachments, readings, workshops and playwriting groups. Twenty years of the International Department's pioneering work around the world means the Royal Court has relationships with writers on every continent.

Within the past sixty years, John Osborne, Samuel Beckett, Arnold Wesker, Ann Jellicoe, Howard Brenton, David Hare and many more started their careers at the Court.

Many others, including Caryl Churchill, Athol Fugard, Mark Ravenhill, Simon Stephens, debbie tucker green and Sarah Kane have followed.

More recently, the theatre has fostered new writers such as Lucy Kirkwood, Nick Payne, Penelope Skinner and Alistair McDowall and produced many iconic plays from Laura Wade's **Posh** to Jez Butterworth's **Jerusalem** and Martin McDonagh's **Hangmen.**

Royal Court plays from every decade are now performed on stage and taught in classrooms and universities across the globe.

It is because of this commitment to the writer that we believe there is no more important theatre in the world than the Royal Court.

Supported using public funding by
ARTS COUNCIL ENGLAND

ROYAL

IN 2016 THE ROYAL COURT IS 60 YEARS NEW

17 May – 21 May
Ophelias Zimmer
Directed by Katie Mitchell
Designed by Chloe Lamford
Text by Alice Birch
In association with Schaubühne Berlin

23 Jun – 13 Jul
Cuttin' It
By Charlene James
A Royal Court/Young Vic co-production
with Birmingham Repertory Theatre,
Sheffield Theatres and The Yard Theatre

1 Jul – 6 Aug
Unreachable
By Anthony Neilson

7 Sep – 15 Oct
Torn
By Nathaniel Martello-White

15 Sep – 22 Oct
Father Comes Home
From The Wars
(Parts 1, 2 & 3)
By Suzan-Lori Parks

Tickets from £10. 020 7565 5000 (no booking fee)
royalcourttheatre.com

JERWOOD **CHARITABLE**
FOUNDATION

Cuttin' It and Torn are part of the Royal Court's
Jerwood New Playwrights programme, supported
by Jerwood Charitable Foundation

Innovation partner
  Supported using public funding by
ARTS COUNCIL
ENGLAND

Sloane Square London, SW1W 8AS
🐦 royalcourt 📘 royalcourttheatre
🚇 Sloane Square ⇌ Victoria Station

COURT

ROYAL COURT SUPPORTERS

The Royal Court is a registered charity and not-for-profit company. We need to raise £1.7 million every year in addition to our core grant from the Arts Council and our ticket income to achieve what we do.

We have significant and longstanding relationships with many generous organisations and individuals who provide vital support. Royal Court supporters enable us to remain the writers' theatre, find stories from everywhere and create theatre for everyone.

We can't do it without you.

Coutts supports Innovation at the Royal Court. The Genesis Foundation supports the Royal Court's work with International Playwrights. Bloomberg supports Beyond the Court. Jerwood Charitable Foundation supports emerging writers through the Jerwood New Playwrights series. The Pinter Commission is given annually by his widow, Lady Antonia Fraser, to support a new commission at the Royal Court.

PUBLIC FUNDING

Arts Council England, London
British Council

CHARITABLE DONATIONS

The Austin & Hope
  Pilkington Trust
Martin Bowley Charitable Trust
The City Bridge Trust
The Clifford Chance
  Foundation
Cockayne - Grants for the Arts
The Ernest Cook Trust
Cowley Charitable Trust
The Dorset Foundation
The Eranda Foundation
Lady Antonia Fraser for
    The Pinter Commission
Genesis Foundation
The Golden Bottle Trust

The Haberdashers' Company
Roderick & Elizabeth Jack
Jerwood Charitable
  Foundation
Kirsh Foundation
The Mackintosh Foundation
Marina Kleinwort Trust
The Andrew Lloyd Webber
  Foundation
The London Community
  Foundation
John Lyon's Charity
Clare McIntyre's Bursary
The Andrew W. Mellon
  Foundation
The Mercers' Company
The Portrack Charitable Trust
The David & Elaine Potter
  Foundation
The Richard Radcliffe
  Charitable Trust
Rose Foundation
Royal Victoria Hall Foundation
The Sackler Trust
The Sobell Foundation
John Thaw Foundation
The Vandervell Foundation
Sir Siegmund Warburg's
  Voluntary Settlement
The Garfield Weston
  Foundation
The Wolfson Foundation

CORPORATE SPONSORS

AKA
AlixPartners
Aqua Financial Solutions Ltd
Bloomberg
Colbert
Coutts
Edwardian Hotels, London
Fever-Tree
Gedye & Sons

Kudos
MAC
Nyetimber

BUSINESS MEMBERS

Auerbach & Steele
  Opticians
CNC – Communications &
  Network Consulting
Cream
Hugo Boss UK
Lansons
Left Bank Pictures
Rockspring Property
  Investment Managers
Tetragon Financial Group
Vanity Fair

DEVELOPMENT COUNCIL

Majella Altschuler
Piers Butler
Sarah Chappatte
Cas Donald
Celeste Fenichel
Piers Gibson
Emma Marsh
Angelie Moledina
Anatol Orient
Andrew Rodger
Deborah Shaw
Sian Westerman

Innovation partner

  ARTS COUNCIL ENGLAND

Supported using public funding by

The Royal Court works with a huge variety of companies ranging from small local businesses to large global firms. The Court has been at the cutting edge of new drama for more than 50 years and, situated in the heart of Chelsea, makes the perfect evening for a night of unique client entertaining.

By becoming a Business Member, your company will be given an allocation of London's hottest tickets with the chance of booking in for sold out shows, the opportunity to entertain your clients in our stunning Balcony Bar and exclusive access to the creative members of staff and cast members.

BECOME A BUSINESS MEMBER

To discuss Business Membership at the Royal Court, please contact:
Nadia Vistisen, Development Officer
nadiavistisen@royalcourttheatre.com
020 7565 5030

LOVE
NEW
WRITING

The English Stage Company at the Royal Court Theatre is a registered charity (No. 231242).

HUMAN ANIMALS

Stef Smith

'Life on earth has often been disturbed by terrible events… living organisms without number have been the victims of these catastrophe… their races are even finished forever, and all they leave behind is some debris.'

Georges Cuvier
Fossil, Bones, and Geological Catastrophes (1796)

'Though it might be nice to imagine there once was a time when man lived in harmony with nature, it's not clear that he ever really did.'

Elizabeth Kolbert
The Sixth Extinction (2014)

Acknowledgements

I would like to thank the incredible cast, crew and creative team who brought *Human Animals* to life in its premiere production in May 2016. Thanks too to the people at the Royal Court who made that possible and were part of that process, especially Vicky Featherstone who never fails to embolden me.

I would also like to thank the following actors for their generosity and invaluable work during the development of the play: Robert Bathurst, Neil Dudgeon, Laura Elphinstone, Matti Houghton, Ferdinand Kingsley, Pepter Lunkuse, Lyndsey Marshal, Sarah Malin, Ferdy Roberts, Justin Salinger, Lesley Sharp and Nathan Stewart-Jarrett.

Special thanks to debbie tucker green for her wise words, rigour, laughter and encouragement during the evolution of this text.

For their support while I was writing and making *Human Animals* I'd also like to thank my agent Davina, Joanna, Louise, Ros & Simon, the Smiths, and of course, Gilly. I'm especially grateful for her love and enthusiasm.

Finally, thank you to Hamish Pirie for his fearlessness, his friendship and his brilliant brain.

S.S.

Author's Note

This play is in chronological order.

A forward slash (/) denotes an interruption.

In the sections where there are lines that are in *italics*, they may be given to any cast member. They can also be spoken simultaneously by multiple performers. Stage directions are given in bold italics.

In the final scene of this play there is a reference to London public transport and Sloane Square, the location of the Royal Court, where the play was first produced. If happening outside of London these references should be changed to similar references that suit the location where the performance is happening. The same can be done to the reference to Edinburgh Castle and Orkney if the performance is taking place outside of the UK.

Where entirely necessary the performers may change words to suit their dialect.

The play should be as grounded and vivid as possible, with each moment finding its own energy, different from the scene before.

Characters

ALEX, *twenties*
JAMIE, *thirties*
JOHN, *fifties*
LISA, *thirties*
NANCY, *fifties*
SI, *forties*

These characters can be any race.

This text went to press before the end of rehearsals and so may differ slightly from the play as performed.

LISA   Was it bleeding when you found it?

JAMIE   No.

LISA   Why is there a tea towel over it? I got that tea
        towel from our trip to Edinburgh Castle. It just
        flew through the window?

JAMIE   I just couldn't... you know... it was just there –
        looking at me. With its beady little eyes. They're
        much smaller than you'd think. Its skull was only
        the size of a matchbox. What do you think it was
        flying from?

LISA   Might have just got confused or lost. Is it a boy or
        a girl?

JAMIE   I don't know how you tell. Do you think it had
        eggs? Like babies?

LISA   Jamie.

JAMIE   Well. There might be chicks out there.

LISA   Are you getting sentimental on me?

JAMIE   No, I'm just... thinking about /

LISA   Are you going to /

JAMIE   No. I'm just... What?

LISA   Nothing. You just surprise me sometimes is all.

JAMIE   Is that a bad thing?

LISA   No... No.

        I don't think I've ever seen a dead pigeon before.

        Are we just going to leave it on our living-room
        floor? How are we going to get blood off the
        carpet?

JAMIE   I'm not picking it up. I've already had to look at
             the thing.

             Silence.

LISA   I'll get the rubber gloves.

JOHN	It's not my fault they're using guns, Nancy!
NANCY	It's your garden, John – the sound is awful and I'm not your only neighbour. You've got the Hendersons the other side and they can be right B-words.

JOHN *smiles.*

Stop looking at me like I'm ridiculous.

JOHN	When was the last time you swore?
NANCY	1987.

I stood on a bee – my foot swelled up to the size of a melon. I imagine I swore then.

The sound of a gunshot fills the room.

JOHN	It's my only option.
NANCY	Couldn't they put some poison down or something?
JOHN	Poison is for rats, not pigeons – plus there was too many of them. Doubling in numbers.
NANCY	Were you scared?
JOHN	It takes more than a few pigeons to scare me.

Okay it was a little frightening. But there were seventy-nine pigeons, three seagulls and two swallows on my last count.

NANCY	Did they say what caused it?
JOHN	Pest control said it has something to do with flocking patterns changing.
NANCY	Do pigeons flock?
JOHN	All I know is there are seventy-nine of the bloody things in the garden shitting on my new decking. Thank God I got that power hose last winter… When is Alex back?

NANCY   She's back on Wednesday, at seven.

JOHN   Remember, she'll be different though, and exactly the same.

NANCY   She sent me these photos last month and she looked so like Richard it's startled me. He'd be so proud of her.

JOHN   You'll be glad when she is back.

NANCY   I wished the garden looks a little more... ready for her return. My poor roses. Never thought a flower would make me feel guilty but I just look out the window and they are there – weeping. It's funny how roses can look like they're weeping. But at least they keep me company.

JOHN   I did wonder the other day if I rather enjoy my own company a little too much.

NANCY   But you're such wonderful company I can see why you wouldn't want anyone else's. I hope Alex hasn't done anything regrettable with her hair. Trips like that do that, don't they? Make people have regrettable hair.

JOHN   My poor sister had to get part of her head shaved – for the stitches last week.

NANCY   Do you think she still loves him? Your sister I mean. Still loves the man who hit her.

JOHN   I imagine so. Love can be like that – can't it. She'll get the stitches out and forget all about it. Like that cat of yours. Poor thing.

NANCY   Down to his last life, silly feline. If it wasn't for Richard having loved the blinking thing so much I would have given him away years ago.

JOHN   Now, that's not true. Is it?

NANCY *rolls her eyes.*

Silence.

NANCY   How's work?

JOHN   Still there. Still paying the bills. Is it too early for
          a G'n'T?

NANCY   No, never. After all gin is clear – it's practically
          water.

JAMIE   'There are five survivors, four normal adult human beings and a dog. The boat will support only four. All will perish if one is not sacrificed. Which one ought to be cast overboard?'

LISA   The dog.

JAMIE   Why?

LISA   Because it's a dog.

JAMIE   What if three of them were in the Nazi Party, and one was a paedophile? And the dog was a Labrador.

LISA   The paedophile.

JAMIE   What if the paedophile was a woman?

          Pause.

LISA   What sort of boat is this?

JAMIE   It's a game. I read it on the internet at work.

LISA   Productive day then?

JAMIE   It was my lunch break. Nazi or paedophile or Labrador?

LISA   Are those my only options?

JAMIE   Go on!

LISA   No! Stop this, I'm tired. I've had a long day.

JAMIE   So have I.

          Pause.

LISA   Well.

          How about I just kiss you.

          Really soft.

          Just here… and here… and here… I always loved your skin.

          Are you going to kiss me back?

JAMIE	Sure. Just here… and here… and here…

They continue to kiss. Time passes.

LISA *notices something and gets distracted.*

LISA	Is there blood on that window?
JAMIE	What?
LISA	Blood on that window?
JAMIE	Can we just /
LISA	When did that happen?
JAMIE	Earlier today. A pigeon.
LISA	Another pigeon flew into the window?
JAMIE	It didn't smash it this time.
LISA	And you didn't think to clean it?
JAMIE	I've been at work.
LISA	You walked through that door an hour ago, you could have cleaned its blood.
JAMIE	Her blood. It was a girl.
LISA	What.
JAMIE	The pigeon – the first one and the second. Females. I looked it up on the internet.
LISA	What did you do with it? Where is the pigeon now?
	Jamie.
JAMIE	I went to take the bins out and I found the pigeon. She was bleeding and crying and so I picked her up and put her in a box.
LISA	And then where did you put that box?
JAMIE	Well, I thought it /
LISA	Where is the pigeon?
JAMIE	It's in a box in the bathroom.

LISA   In our bathroom?

JAMIE   It's the warmest room in the house. I'm nursing it. The thing obviously wants to live. It would have died if it didn't want to live. I've got a lot of respect for pigeons.

LISA   Well I don't.

JAMIE   There was a fox as well, in amongst the bins. Now that was dead. Fresh dead, it was still soft.

LISA   You touched it?

JAMIE   Just with a stick.

        I felt bad for it. So I dug it a grave.

LISA   Are you telling me there is a fox buried in my garden?

JAMIE   It's our garden.

LISA   Couldn't you have just left it where you found it?

JAMIE   I had to do something with it.

LISA   No you didn't! Normal people just leave dead animals. I hope you washed your hands before touching anything.

JAMIE   I was trying to be respectful.

LISA   I'm not sure foxes give a shit about respect and it's not the fox's garden.

JAMIE   Well maybe it is.

LISA   What?

JAMIE   Maybe, just maybe a fox and his kids lived there, hundreds of years ago and then we came along and fucked it up for him. I mean I would say he has a right to be buried there, on his great-grandfather's father's land, on his ancestors' land.

LISA   Is this really what you're saying?

JAMIE   What I'm saying is that fox – out there – has a right to be buried wherever he wants.

LISA   Fine! Fine, Jamie. Whatever.

But.

Don't go burying wild animals in my garden.

Or at least ask for permission first.

JAMIE   Or what?

LISA   You are lucky you look handsome when you're all worked up.

LISA *kisses him, first playfully then hard.*

JAMIE   The thing with the fox is /

LISA   I think they're eyeing me up for a manager's job. If I get it – and I mean if – I am kicking the arse out of our anniversary weekend away.

JAMIE   It's not for another month.

LISA   I'm just saying… Maybe I'll buy us a tiramisu. Will you make dinner tonight?

Go on…

She kisses him.

JAMIE   What's in it for me?

She smiles.

SI   I think you dropped this.

JOHN   Excuse me.

SI   Handkerchief. On the bathroom floor. It looks like silk so I /

JOHN   Thank you.

SI   Is that blood on it?

            Pause.

JOHN   Nosebleed.

SI   A lot of blood for a nosebleed.

            That shade of blue is unusual.

JOHN   Robin's egg. It's called Robin's egg.

SI   Are you… gay?

JOHN   What did you say?

SI   Are you gay?

JOHN   I'm not going to answer that.

SI   I don't mean it in a bad way.

            Pause.

            Sorry.

            Let me buy you a drink. I didn't mean to /

JOHN   A pint of anything heavy.

SI   Sorry?

JOHN   I'll drink a pint of anything heavy… Something bitter, strong and dark. Bonus points if it's Scottish. I've always had a soft spot for the Scots.

SI   Okay.

JAMIE	Why are you looking at me like that?
	What?
	Silence.
LISA	Nothing, it's nothing.
JAMIE	Lisa.
LISA	I just got a really overwhelming need to fuck you.
	Right here on the carpet.
	Do you ever get that?
JAMIE	Sure.
LISA	Pheromones or something.
JAMIE	Well… I mean… Don't let me stop you.
	Silence.
LISA	Okay then.

NANCY   Let me do your washing.

ALEX   No, it's okay.

NANCY   Honestly, it's not a bother.

           You're an old soul. Your father used to say that.

ALEX   Are you saying I've got wrinkles?

NANCY   No. You've beautiful skin.

ALEX   Have you had your hair done?

NANCY   Just a little off the ends.

ALEX   It looks nice.

NANCY   You look cold. Do you want me to turn on the heating?

ALEX   No, it's fine.

NANCY   Do you want me to run you a bath? Baths are great for jetlag.

ALEX   No, honestly. It's fine.

NANCY   If you need anything /

ALEX   How about – I make dinner for us tonight.

NANCY   But I /

ALEX   I'll do it.

NANCY   No it's just that /

ALEX   We both know my chicken is better.

NANCY   Fine.

           But be careful going into the freezer in the garage. It's full of pigeons.

ALEX   What?

NANCY   Pigeons. The ones from John's garden. He said I could make a stew but... I mean what would you serve with them? Potatoes? Grandma always used to say a meal isn't a meal unless it's with potatoes.

ALEX *goes to leave.*

Oh don't go out there!

ALEX   What?! I'm going to get the cat.

NANCY   We shouldn't go in the back garden.

ALEX   Why?

NANCY   It's just until environmental control have made sure there aren't any foxes in our shrubs.

They said we shouldn't go near their bodies. Something happened with a little girl down the road but honestly – it's just a case of hysteria.

And anyway, saves me having to hang out the washing.

Why do you look so sad?

Silence.

ALEX   Not sad.

I'm just...

I'd like to find a way – a way to be more... over here. There are plenty of things that need doing. Plenty of people who need... I thought I might find a way... a way to... be useful.

NANCY   That's nice.

Silence.

What are we going to do about the cat?

Blood dries darker than you think

It's that moment of darkness into deeper darkness

Are those my only options?

Congealed red on the glass

A mouse in your / cereal box

A noise / up ahead

A scratching / between the wall

As they shot them right / through the wing

Are you going to kiss me back?

Are you going to?

Scratching.

Are you going?

Scurrying.

Are you?

Screaming.

Are you going to?

Scratching.

Are you going?

Scurrying.

Are you?

Screaming.

Scratching.

Scurrying.

Screaming.

What was that noise?

LISA   I said two days – max. Your forty-eight hours
          are up.

JAMIE   I don't think she will survive if I let her go. She's
          fragile, she's life-and-death fragile. I picked her
          up, now she's my responsibility. Please.

LISA   Why do you care so much?

JAMIE   Why don't you?

LISA   Because I don't have time to care or the energy!

JAMIE   You could /

LISA   When was the last time you bought me flowers?

JAMIE   What?

LISA   When was the last time you bought me flowers?

JAMIE   I don't know maybe your /

LISA   In the past two days you've paid more attention to
          that fucking pigeon than me.

JAMIE   I didn't mean /

LISA   In a parallel universe somewhere we would be
          having a baby, Jamie. If that little stick last month
          had shown two blue lines would you be as fussed
          about a pigeon with a fucked wing.

JAMIE   No, of course not I... I'm just /

LISA   I'm here, Jamie. I'm right fucking here.

          You said last month you said you'd take me out
          for a plush dinner. Plush! And I remember that
          because I thought it was weird that you'd used the
          word plush – I remember thinking – who the fuck
          uses the word plush but then I also thought – yeah,
          lovely. I'd love a plush dinner, we work hard, we
          work hard so we can do nice things. But we still

haven't done nice things, Jamie, we haven't done nice things in a long time.

Silence.

JAMIE   I'm sorry. I figured since we've got our anniversary coming up…

LISA   I know. I just…

JAMIE   We can go out for dinner tonight if you want?

NANCY *is whistling/cooing as if she is calling an animal.*

NANCY   He hasn't touched his breakfast.

ALEX   He'll just be out.

NANCY   It's not like him to miss a meal.

               NANCY *continues to whistle for the cat.*

ALEX   Why don't you ask John?

NANCY   He's at work.

               Mr Marmalade! Mr Marmalade!

ALEX   He doesn't need to be called mister.

NANCY   What would you know about cats?

               Pause.

ALEX   Mr Marmalade!

               He's probably out impregnating some poor female.

NANCY   Alexandra! Mr Marmalade isn't like that.

ALEX   Yes. He is.

NANCY   I've often wondered if Mr Marmalade rather
               likes... boy cats more than girl cats.

ALEX   Can cats be /

NANCY   Don't see why not. I'll ask John.

ALEX   Why would John know?

NANCY   John knows everything about homosexual
               lifestyles.

               Did you meet a boy?

ALEX   What?

NANCY   Did you meet a boy on your trip? Or a girl – I
               don't mind... I can be, you know.

               Silence.

I knew it. I can smell romance a mile away. What was his – her – his name?

ALEX   It doesn't matter what *her* name was. It was nothing serious.

NANCY   *Her* name? I didn't realise you were /

ALEX   It honestly doesn't matter.

NANCY   I mean… is this something we need to talk about?

ALEX   Please don't make it into a thing.

NANCY   If I know one thing it's that it's always love at your age… and if you're… with a… Marmalade!

ALEX   It was just a fling.

NANCY   When I was your age I was expecting you.

ALEX   Have you ever thought about travelling?

NANCY   Of course I've thought about it but thinking about it and doing it are two very different things. Plus it just won't be the same without your father.

ALEX   You should treat yourself, they do these organised /

NANCY   I haven't the time for a holiday. Plus what would John do? Mr Marmalade! Cat biscuits!

ALEX   You don't have to /

NANCY   Speaking of which I called John, he said they're starting a fire in those bushes by the shop. Something to do with foxes.

ALEX   They can't just start burning /

NANCY   It's only a patch of turf. Plus they burnt that warehouse down last year, the one near your father's old work. And that didn't even make it into the newspaper, I only found out because I went to visit your father's old office and all there was left was ash and police tape.

ALEX   They can't just do that.

NANCY   Of course they can. They can do whatever they
            want if it makes people safe. I mean I feel safer
            already.

ALEX   Why were you at Dad's old office?

NANCY   Sometimes I drive past it.

            Maybe once or twice I've even parked in the
            car park.

            I like that it reminds me of him. There I said it.

            Silence.

            Marmalade!

SI   I thought you only came here on Fridays.

JOHN   The road is shut. Something to do with the dogs.

            Which is tedious.

SI   Just finished work have you?

            Silence.

            What did the farmer say to the horse?

JOHN   Why the long face?

SI   You've heard it?

JOHN   What do you think?

SI   That's my daughter's favourite joke.

JOHN   It's not very /

SI   I said that's my daughter's favourite joke.

JOHN   …Good one.

            Silence.

SI   She doesn't live with me, my daughter. What have you got?

JOHN   Nothing. I don't have… children.

SI   I've got another joke for you /

JOHN   I'm not really into 'jokes'.

SI   You don't like laughing?

JOHN   That's not what I said.

SI   You might as well have.

JOHN   I just don't like jokes.

SI   You haven't heard it yet, you might like this joke.

JOHN   Thank you but no thank you.

SI   Are you sure?

JOHN   Utterly.

SI   It's a pity. It was a really funny joke.

ALEX   I saw something about a kid being bitten by a
              fox… she might have rabies or something like it…
              Aren't you even a little bit worried, with all this?
              Everything that's happening?

NANCY   Not particularly, when you've lived a few years –
              which I have – you get used to these things
              happening every now and again.

ALEX   It's a lot to come back to – isn't it?

NANCY   Things happen whether you're here or not.

ALEX   I know that… I just mean…

NANCY   You'll get used to it again. You're very…
              adaptable.

LISA   Why are you looking at me like that?

            What?

            Silence.

JAMIE   Nothing, it's nothing.

LISA   Jamie.

JAMIE   I just got a really overwhelming need to fuck you.

            Right here on the carpet.

            Do you ever get that?

LISA   Sure.

JAMIE   Pheromones or something.

LISA   Well... I mean... Don't let me stop you.

            Silence.

JAMIE   Okay then.

JOHN   Did your mother never tell you not to talk to strangers?

SI   I'm trying to be your friend.

JOHN   Why?

SI   Because that's what people do, isn't it.

JOHN   No. It's not.

SI   You drink in this pub so you can talk to me.

JOHN   I drink in this pub because it's on my walk home from work.

SI   You can be my friend if you want.

JOHN   No thank you.

SI   That's not a nice thing to say to a friend, John.

    Pause.

JOHN   How do you know my name?

    They're quietly pouring petrol on the bushes

SI   I'm just looking for some company.

    And they'll light them at night

    So no one has to know.

JOHN   I think you better look somewhere else.

The sound of birds calling

Mice are chewing through their own veins

            I can't stop watching

        Frogs are calmly laying eggs in cold baths
            I can't stop watching

        Dead flies all along the window ledge
            I can't stop watching

I can't.

Is that the smell of skin burning?

A body of a dead mouse rolls across the floor of the bus

> *The smell of stagnant water*

> *A child cries somewhere a little too close*

A dog yelps and snaps

The sound of metal on metal and glass and screaming
and crying
and screaming
and then silence

JOHN   What are these?

NANCY   I've been taking the cat's Prozac.

JOHN   What?

           But it's not the type of silence that feels like a void,
           a nothingness, it's the type of silence that is so
           thick it makes you choke.

NANCY   The cat got depressed after Richard died. The vet
           said they're surprisingly emotional creatures.

JOHN   Well I can understand that.

NANCY   So he got a prescription for Prozac.

JOHN   Is it the same as humans'?

NANCY   I hope so.

JOHN   And it's helped? With... well...

NANCY   It's helped. I'm finding it all a little overwhelming.

JOHN   They'll open the road again. I don't understand
           why you don't talk to me.

NANCY   I see you once a week, John! We talk!

JOHN   But if you feel sad. And if you're... I mean.

NANCY   I've had quite enough of sadness. Haven't you?

           Now. Are you pouring the drinks or am I?

LISA   I don't like that wild thing being in here.

JAMIE   I never complained about your friends coming over.

LISA   Jamie. The thing is just going to die in that box – at least let it die out there.

JAMIE   It'll get eaten by a fox if I let it go like that – and that's a horrible way to go.

LISA   It's not sanitary. They're handing out these leaflets.

JAMIE   You mean those home-printed pieces of nonsense?

LISA   It says you shouldn't touch any non-domesticated wildlife. That includes pigeons and foxes. See, there is a fox, right there on the front.

JAMIE   I rescued the pigeon before all this.

LISA   How do you know it's not infected?

JAMIE   Infected with what?

LISA   They're worried people can get it.

JAMIE   Get what!

LISA   Whatever it is that's making the birds and the foxes and the rats crazy.

JAMIE   Oh, heaven forbid the animals are acting like animals. I'm more scared of humans than foxes. That's the truth.

LISA   I don't want you getting sick.

JAMIE   It's fine. Honestly. Looking after that bird is the most useful thing I've done in months. At work I'm barely pushing paper around a table – but this… I'm not stupid, I know when something is sick. That bird isn't sick.

              Plus you always wanted a pet.

LISA   That's a lie... Though I wouldn't say no to one of
            those labradoodles... you know the dog that's a
            cross between a Labrador and a poodle /

JAMIE   I know what it is... they're pretty cute – I'll give
            you that. It's something about how their ears...
            that's just /

LISA   I mean you're not even a vegetarian.

JAMIE   It's not my fault I'm allergic to tofu.

            In my next life I'm coming back as a fox because
            frankly it would be easier than being a human.

LISA   You'd be a terrible fox.

JAMIE   I'm resourceful.

LISA   Yeah, but you don't suit orange.

            If it's going to make you that sad – keep the bloody
            pigeon. But if it's not dead in a week or for one
            minute I think it looks sick – you're letting it go.

            Deal?

JAMIE   Deal.

LISA   Do you think we should get a puppy?

NANCY	You look a little flushed, sweetheart – are you feeling okay?
ALEX	I'm fine – just tired.
JOHN	You saw my name on my credit card.
SI	So?
JOHN	That's how you knew my name. My credit card sticks out the side of my wallet. See... I figured you out.
SI	Was that keeping you awake at night?
NANCY	Are you sure?
	I don't want you getting sick.
	I've got a leaflet on the symptoms.
JOHN	My privacy matters a great deal to me. It bothers me when I think it's been compromised.
SI	I'm a private man too. I've got plenty of secrets. Full of secrets, me.
JOHN	You don't intrigue me.
SI	No?
ALEX	I'm fine.
NANCY	But /
ALEX	I'm fine.

Silence.

SI	You'll want to keep a hold of that credit card – rumour has it they are closing the banks now they've started shutting some of the roads. Maybe they are worried people will riot and turn on the banks. People are always so angry at the banks... have you noticed?
	Funny to think this all just started with some foxes.

JOHN   I never much cared for animals but I certainly didn't want them to die these appalling deaths... being burnt alive is a terrible way to go.

Do you think it's to do with overpopulation?

SI   Considering vegetarianism are you?

Pause.

My round.

ALEX   I mean really it's all down to the guy that ran the charity. He was just brilliant. He's been vaccinating people for twenty-five years.

NANCY   Oh you think he'd get bored.

ALEX   Mum /

NANCY   What? It's a joke… What was the most beautiful thing you saw?

ALEX   Probably a wild dolphin.

NANCY   A dolphin! Your father always wanted to see dolphins in real life. The closest thing we got to them was a dead seal on a beach in Orkney. They have just got a dolphin for that aquarium near where Grandma used to live. You should go and see it – when they open the roads.

ALEX   It's not the same though is it.

NANCY   For all you know that dolphin is having a bloody wonderful time.

ALEX   Even you know that /

NANCY   Are there any nibbles?

ALEX   No. Should I go to the shop for more Bombay mix?

NANCY   Oh, you shouldn't. Curfew.

          They've put a recommended curfew on the street. From dusk till dawn while they hunt out the foxes. It's only recommended but I think it's worth being careful.

ALEX   Are you kidding me?

NANCY   Do you want to catch whatever it is going about? I don't. They say you can get it just by looking at a fox now.

ALEX   That's bullshit /

NANCY   Watch your language.

ALEX   You can't go around not looking at animals.

NANCY   Well I'm willing to try.

ALEX   So we're stuck?

NANCY   I'm not sure you can ever really be described as
          stuck when you're surrounded by double glazing.
          Plus there is vodka from Christmas.

ALEX   Maybe we could go away for the weekend? What
          do you think? While all this passes? Me and you
          could... just get away. Maybe go somewhere on
          the coast?

NANCY   But what if the cat comes back and we aren't here?

ALEX   I don't think he will /

NANCY   I'll think about it, sweetheart.

ALEX   I just need to – I can't just sit around... I can't
          just... I've spent the last few months seeing the
          most... being the most... but the most useful thing
          I've done today is make a gin and tonic.

NANCY   That's not my fault is it?

ALEX   I think it would be good for us to get away. Just
          get away.

NANCY   How *is* the job-hunt going?

LISA   She talked enough about things, it didn't feel like
          she didn't talk about things. I mean we weren't
          that close... she just sat opposite me. I remember
          last week she seemed panicked. She is scared of
          birds you see, scared of pigeons and she had
          walked into a stack of their bodies in her bathroom
          – they've flown through the window. She showed
          me a picture on her phone.

          Pause.

ALEX   I've sent out nearly twenty CVs, Mum. I'm trying…

               I'd like to start paying rent. Start… helping out around /

NANCY   Finding comfort jarring. Are you?

ALEX   What is that supposed to mean?

               Silence.

NANCY   The vodka's in the cupboard next to the cooker.

               Pause.

LISA   I never thought about how easy it is to… I know it's glib but… but it's just… easy.

JAMIE   I'm not sure that's true. When it comes down to it.

LISA   I passed a bin on fire on my walk home… smelt like burning hair.

JAMIE   It'll be the foxes. They're burning the foxes.

LISA   Makes me want to see my mum… all of this. Makes me think of my mum.

JAMIE   Makes me want to leave my job.

               They're making us wear face masks now – and it's only a fucking call centre. They're worried about the cockroaches we had last year. They're worried they will come back and they'll be infected. We're just fucking minimum-wage morons to those guys in charge. If it was that dangerous they should close the building. We're treated like cattle.

LISA   At work they're making us dip our shoes in these little trays of /

JAMIE   They're just being overcautious.

               Silence.

LISA   I need for you to tell me you love me. Every day.

JAMIE   I love you.

LISA   And you've got to tell me tomorrow and the day
           after and the day after and the day after. Until you
           don't love me any more or one of us is dead.

JAMIE   Okay.

ALEX   I need for you to know I love you.

LISA   I love you.

NANCY   Of course I know that, darling.

JAMIE   I love you.

NANCY   I love you too.

LISA   I don't want to kill myself.

JAMIE   That's a reasonable thought.

LISA   Can you hug me please?

JOHN   I don't think your eyes are that squinty.

SI   I swear. People think I'm bad because I've got squinty eyes.

JOHN   I think your eyes seem... quite... typical. But I'm not an optometrist.

SI   What is it you do?

JOHN   I organise.

SI   Organise what?

JOHN   Things and people.

SI   No more details?

JOHN   No more details.

SI   They've closed the roads going over the water. Something to do with spores.

JOHN   I'm sure it's fine.

SI   My daughter lives over there. It was my weekend to have her.

JOHN   Sorry.

SI   You don't seem sorry.

JOHN   Well I am.

SI   Have you seen the pictures of the barricades on the road? People tweeting them. Just feet away from those piles of burning animals. Foxes and dogs and pigeons. You ever seen the inside of a Labrador? Horrible – photo just flashed up on my Facebook and /

JOHN   Please.

         Don't.

ALEX	They can't just burn it down – a whole park.
NANCY	It's only a park. They need to get rid of the foxes' habitats. Somehow.
ALEX	It's not – only a park.
NANCY	I know. It's that park your father loved. He used to take you there.
ALEX	We put some of his ashes there.
NANCY	Only half a teaspoon. It doesn't matter.

NANCY   You're overreacting.

ALEX   Dad would have gone and protested if he was here.

NANCY   No he wouldn't have. Your father hated crowds.

Plus – above all he was a realist, Alex. A realist, not an idealist like you.

ALEX   No. He would have been the first one there. Because he taught me to ride a bike in it and because every Christmas Eve we would go and he'd let me have a couple of draws on his cigar and then tell me never to take up smoking. And we'd laugh, we'd sit on a bench and we'd laugh.

You're wrong. You're wrong. He'd be the first one there saying – this park belongs to me and my daughter. Because he loved me and he loved that park. Because I loved him, and I loved that park.

I go there to visit him.

That's how I remember him.

I'm not letting them take that from me.

It's all I have left!

NANCY   Frankly, Alex. You don't have a choice.

Don't look at me like that. I know that you're so... restless. I know how you miss him.

ALEX   No. You don't.

            You never had any idea.

NANCY   What do you mean?

ALEX   I mean – I don't want to be anything like you.

NANCY   Good.

SI	Have you ever had someone? Someone special?
JOHN	Yes.
SI	Do you miss them?
JOHN	Not particularly.
SI	I think you're nice company.
JOHN	And I think you want something…
SI	No.
	I really just think you're /
JOHN	You are a very strange fellow.
	Has anyone ever said that?
SI	No.
	My ex-wife used to say I was inscrutable.
	But I rather took that as a compliment.
	Even at the end.
JOHN	And what is she like?
SI	Vile.
	She is mostly vile.

JAMIE   I quit.

LISA   You what?

JAMIE   I quit. I pissed on the boss's laptop. Ex-boss's laptop.

LISA   You what?

JAMIE   Well. I pissed in a cup and then poured it on his laptop and handed in my notice. They were scared to do anything about it in case I hurt myself – because that guy in marketing last week... I handed in my notice and walked out. I'm the fourth person to quit this week. Everyone is /

LISA   You're not /

JAMIE   I just couldn't... because it was so... and I was so...

It's that feeling of breathlessness... Just here.

Here. Can you feel it?

He takes her hand, presses it against his chest.

I'm sorry.

Silence.

LISA   Why didn't you say something before?

JAMIE   I'd gotten used to how shit it was... I'd just stopped seeing it.

And then with everything that's happened... it's all I could see.

LISA   This is a lot to land on me.

JAMIE   I'll make it work. I promise. I just need... please don't be... I stayed as long as I could but... I was totally utterly... desperate. I suppose I was desperate.

NANCY   If you feel a little lost, darling /

ALEX   I don't feel lost.

I just…

I'm going for a walk.

NANCY   Well be careful!

SI   You don't look well – are you sick?

JOHN   Please.

            You're overwhelming me with your compliments.

            I'm having to get up an hour early to take a
            different route into work. They've closed the road
            I take.

SI   I know.

            I work in chemical distribution.

            We've done three hundred and twenty-four per
            cent more business than usual.

JOHN   That's alarmingly precise.

            So that's why you've got smug written across your
            face. Is it actually killing whatever this thing is?

SI   All I know is that it makes people feel safe.

JAMIE   I was thinking this might be a good time. Help
with what's happening. With everything that's
happening out there.

LISA   So what – you're volunteering?

JAMIE   Something like that.

Do something useful. Like with the pigeon in
the box.

LISA   What that pigeon that died, Jamie. How are we
going to pay the bills?

JAMIE   I've got savings /

LISA   That's not enough.

JAMIE   But maybe it could be enough. I could make sure
it's enough – for now.

Please trust me. I know what I'm asking of you, I
know.

But please.

Silence.

Is there more blood on the window?

LISA   It's doves. These big white doves. Crashing into
the glass.

ALEX   It's like a feeling.

           Just here.

NANCY   Like heartburn?

ALEX   Maybe…

           Maybe it's heartburn.

SI   You'll have to be careful, they're going to close
            the roads heading east. They're going to slowly
            close the roads until we are all just... stuck.

JOHN   That's nonsense.

SI   They're trapping everyone in this postcode, John.
            I'd stock up on groceries if I was you. It'll take a
            while, of course. But until they figure out how to
            deal with it – they trap it in. They'll trap us in. I've
            seen the paperwork.

JOHN   If that's true, how can you be so calm about this?
            What about your daughter?

SI   I'm helping them clean it up. The sooner they
            clean it up the sooner I can get to her.

JOHN   And if you can't?

SI   I'm choosing not to be scared. I recommend you
            do the same.

JOHN   I call bullshit. They can't do half of what you're
            saying. They'll fight it and get rid of it and life
            will tick on as normal.

SI   Little parts of the world go wrong all the time,
            John.

                    *An influx of cats and dogs and bumblebees
                    and bats*

SI   And no one cares.

                    Cats and dogs and bumblebees and bats

SI   Fancy another?

                    Cats and dogs

JOHN   Sure.

                    And centipedes

SI   And don't ever bring up my daughter again.

That is not what we – me and you – do, that's not what this is.

> *And slugs*
>
> *And snails*
>
> *And these teeth like*
>
> *I lie in bed at night and hear the foxes fucking*

JOHN   Don't ever tell me what I can and can't do.

That's not what this is.

And slugs

> *And snails*
>
> > *And these teeth like*
> >
> > > *I lie in bed at night and hear the foxes fucking*

And slugs

> *And snails*
>
> > *And these teeth like*
> >
> > > *I lie in bed at night and hear the foxes fucking*

Are you going to kiss me back?

This is an / early warning.

> *Consider this is an early warning.*
>
> > *No one said*
> >
> > > *No one said evolution was precise*

JOHN   She just wants what is best for you.

ALEX   I know.

JOHN   Work experience could help.

ALEX   But what's the point?

JOHN   It might not be as worthy as what you were doing
            before but /

ALEX   You think what I was doing out there was *worthy*?

JOHN   I mean /

ALEX   But it's not a job – that's what you're saying. Well,
            I've got news for you, careers don't exist any
            more. It's not like that anywhere. Plus take a look
            outside /

JOHN   Is my work not good enough for you? You want to
            save the world? Is that it?

ALEX   Is that such a bad thing?

JOHN   Let me know when you figure out how.

            Something tells me you'll be a while.

ALEX   Can't you see? How fucked up it all is?

JOHN   I see injustice; I see pain but I fear that's just part
            of it. That's just part of being human.

ALEX   I think it will only get worse out there.

JOHN   You really believe that?

ALEX   Yes. Soon you won't have a work to go to.

JOHN   And so what do we do?

ALEX   I've no idea.

SI	Congratulations.
LISA	Thank you. I really appreciate it. It's unexpected. My… well.
SI	Even as we expand we are looking to keep a community feel to the company – people in this postcode. So it felt right to move you to manager.
LISA	I'm your person.
SI	Great.
LISA	Si?
SI	Yes.
LISA	With the current situation…
SI	Yes?
LISA	How long do you think it will go on for you?
SI	Fingers crossed we can go back to relative normality in a few weeks or so. I've got family commitments the other side of the blockade and a little girl who needs a birthday present.
LISA	Is it true people are getting sick?
SI	Hysteria does funny things to folk. Personally, I take anything with a pinch of salt.
LISA	And the animals? Population control. How many will they have to kill?
SI	All of them. No one likes foxes anyway.
	Oh and we'll be investing in some incinerators soon.
	I think it will be good for business.

NANCY   I'm not letting you do this.

ALEX   You can't stop me.

NANCY   Chaining yourself to the park is not the answer.
          What if they light it, what if they set it on fire
          regardless of you – and you're there. Stuck to
          a railing.

ALEX   It's not just me. There are other people too, other
          people chaining themselves to those iron fences
          because there isn't proof. There isn't proof that
          burning the park will help. People are tweeting
          pictures, people are putting stuff on the internet.
          Posting healthy animals in that park. Just
          yesterday some ducklings hatched and this guy
          posted this photo with them all /

NANCY   Children play in that park. Do you want more
          children getting sick? They've started closing
          schools, Alex. They're worried it might be in the
          soil now, and if it's in the soil it's in the water.

ALEX   That's not true. The newspapers are fear-
          mongering. You know they've wanted that park
          gone for years. It's valuable land. Land where they
          can build shopping malls and flats. It's just an
          excuse. They're spreading fear to get what they
          want. It's what they always do.

NANCY   Why should I believe your idea against what
          everyone else is saying? Frankly, I think they
          should burn all the parks to the ground!

ALEX   Oh shut the fuck up!

NANCY   What did I say about swearing!

          Silence.

          It's just you and me now. It's just the two of us.

ALEX   I know it is. That's why I'm here. That's why I'm in
            this fucking country, to be with you! This isn't as
            selfish as you're making it out. It's bigger than both
            of us. I know it's hard, I know all of this is hard.

NANCY   And you are telling me this now, just before you
            leave. Is this dramatic enough for you? Does this
            make you enough of a martyr?

ALEX   I'm not being a martyr.

NANCY   You're right. You're being a brat.

ALEX   I won't have you talk to me like that. I'm not
            a child.

NANCY   Oh you've made that very clear.

ALEX   They are building a fence around this whole area.
            A chicken-wire fence with barbed wire all
            wrapped into it. So nothing and no one can get out
            – they are trapping us in. How can you see that –
            how can you see that and… live with it. I need to
            do something.

NANCY   No, you don't.

ALEX   I have /

NANCY   Oh, enough. Just leave. Get your things and leave.

JOHN   Would you like a handkerchief?

Silence.

SI   I'm not crying.

JOHN   No?

LISA   Is it you or me who is cooking tonight?

            …hello? You or me?

JAMIE   I'll do it.

            I just need to finish this.

LISA   What are you doing with that hammer?

JAMIE   I'm building.

LISA   Are you fixing that window?

JAMIE   No.

LISA   Well, just as long as you're doing something
            useful…

JAMIE   I meant to say this morning – Happy Anniversary.

LISA   It's not quite the weekend away we were planning.

JAMIE   Can't be helped… can it.

LISA   No.

JAMIE   Bit shit isn't it.

LISA   Yeah… yeah. Pretty shit.

JOHN   You miss your daughter?

         Silence.

SI   They've cut the phone lines because of those
         protests.

         And my signal is becoming patchy now.

JOHN   I know.

         I tried to call my sister… but… I didn't even get a
         dial tone.

LISA	I don't want a bunch of foxes cooped up in the back garden.
	Why can't you just go and volunteer.
JAMIE	This is volunteering!
LISA	No. This is just an internet search that got out of control. Do you know where my keys are?
JAMIE	Don't you get it? This is my chance to stop something, stop something before it's gone too far because frankly everything else has already gone too fucking far.
	I don't understand why you won't help me? Can't you see how important this is?
LISA	I can't understand why you'd take the risk.
JAMIE	It's not that simple any more.
LISA	For me, it is.
JAMIE	Because of your work? Because they are part of /
LISA	Someone has to pay the rent.
JAMIE	I don't know how you can work there.
LISA	I do.
JAMIE	I could make a life that's good for both of us... I can find a way through this. It's just a different way of living... you know... it's just... You don't believe me?
LISA	You're an optimist.
JAMIE	So? That doesn't make me foolish. Hope doesn't make me foolish. Being hopeful is about the bravest thing you can do these days so don't you dare look at me like I'm foolish.
LISA	This isn't the time for big decisions.

JAMIE   It's exactly the time for big decisions.

LISA   Great, I'm late now.

SI   There is nothing worse than having a child's
            bedroom done up perfectly and no one to occupy it.

            I'm going to buy her a guinea pig when all of this
            is over.

JOHN   How's work?

SI   How's yours? Still get there can you?

JOHN   I'm taking some time to work from home.

SI   Don't say I didn't tell you.

            SI *coughs*.

            SI *coughs even harder*.

            What?

JOHN   No it's just… could you cover your mouth?

SI   Why?

            They said it's not airborne.

JOHN   How do you know you've not got it?

SI   I don't.

            Do you miss your /

JOHN   You like asking questions don't you.

            I think I've had enough of questions today.

            Or at least – I've had enough of your questions
            today.

LISA   We're fucking out of apple sauce.

JAMIE   What are you doing?

LISA   I'm baking.

JAMIE   You're baking?

LISA   It's the end of the month which means it's Sweet-Tooth Friday at work and it's my turn. It's my turn and so I'm baking.

JAMIE   This isn't exactly the time for cupcakes /

LISA   I'm making peanut-butter cookies. You use apple sauce instead of eggs.

            I fucking miss eggs.

JAMIE   I think people at work will understand if /

LISA   But it's my turn.

JAMIE   I think people will understand if you can't make a cake. The supermarkets are barely /

LISA   No one else has missed their turn. I'll be damned if I'm going to be the one who fucked up Sweet-Tooth Friday.

JAMIE   Don't be ridiculous.

LISA   I am not being ridiculous. In a couple of weeks' time, it will be like this whole thing never fucking happened and all I want to do is bake fucking peanut-butter cookies.

JAMIE   It won't go back to normal.

LISA   How the hell do you know?

            Try as you might you can't predict the future. And I just got this promotion, Jamie. I've been waiting to be made manager for six years. Six years I worked my way up. I'm the first person in my family to have a full-time job since my granddad and he was essentially a professional drunk. So this stuff – this stuff – you are so quick to dismiss – is important to me.

JAMIE   I know it is.

LISA   Plus the only reason you can continue on your little crusade is because I'm paying the rent. I go to the shop. I change the sheets. So I'm sorry. I'm sorry if I am not as radical as you are – but I need to keep my shit together.

One last time – do you know where the apple sauce is?

JAMIE   Stop being so fucking naive. Haven't you noticed how quiet it is? I haven't heard birds sing in weeks. It's just so quiet. Especially around 5 a.m. They used to sing then. But nothing… now it's just… silence.

You have to let go of the thought that normality will return.

LISA   No I don't. I won't.

JAMIE   Yesterday I sat and watched two men in hazard suits come and pick up all these tiny little bird corpses, and they just threw them into bins. And then I watched them set all the trees on fire. They walked in with these big blowtorches. They were gone as quickly as they came. And I don't think one person looked up. People can get used to terrible things, very quickly. If they have to. It doesn't take much for things to start to fall apart.

Silence.

And I miss the way you used to talk with your hands. You don't do that any more. You've become so… still.

LISA   Fuck you.

A scene with no dialogue.

We see **ALEX** *open a hip flask and take a huge drink.*

She coughs from the strength of the spirit.

There is a release to her actions, an empowerment, a fire.

NANCY   What's this?

JOHN   It's a rap album.

NANCY   You do know you are middle-aged, don't you?
          And a musicals fan.

JOHN   I have an eclectic music taste. So sue me.

NANCY   Why ever would you like... I can't even say the
          title out loud, John! It's so rude...

JOHN   A man can't listen to show tunes alone... I felt...
          and I wanted... I mean it's not music for all the
          time, but after a bottle of Shiraz... why not.

          What? Don't look at me like that. No one ever
          died from a fleeting interest in rap. Now, how
          about that hair of the dog?

NANCY   Do you want to listen to some 'rap' while we drink?

JOHN   Don't make fun.

          Pause.

          How is Alex? It's been days since /

NANCY   As far as I know she is still there. Fighting the
          wind.

JOHN   You know you must give her a little credit for her
          courage. It's been a while since /

NANCY   Do you need your glass filled?

          Time passes.

          Is it strange to make a toast on the anniversary of
          your husband's death? Is it terribly morbid?

          Such nice champagne as well.

          Silence.

          I miss him. It's been four years and I miss Richard
          dreadfully.

JOHN   I think that's understandable. You were married for three decades.

NANCY   It's funny after a while people just sort of expect you to get on. Don't they? You should just get on with it. Like grief is a finite thing, but it's not. True grief lasts for ever and it makes life so terribly impossible.

JOHN   They are heavy words, Nancy.

NANCY   No, John. I fear they are just the right words.

Time passes.

You can see the smoke from them burning that station. Can't remember the last time I got a bus.

JOHN   Was it mice?

NANCY   No. Bluebottles. There is so much ash on everything these days.

I hope they don't burn the library. Richard always loved the architecture of that building.

How many have died?

JOHN   People?

I don't know.

It's rolling blackouts now, even in the afternoon. Rolling blackouts.

NANCY   Then we'll need to get used to the darkness.

Time passes.

JOHN   Have you ever thought about sleeping with me?

NANCY   No.

Well.

Not in a long time.

JOHN   Nanc/

I...

NANCY   I love you, John. I hope you know that.

JOHN   It was never in doubt.

NANCY   Gosh, when did the world get so strange?

JOHN   When people stopped noticing.

Time passes.

NANCY   I wouldn't be too worried though.

SI	We are implementing new regulations.
LISA	Why?
SI	We are increasing the concentration. Make sure you wear a mask in the warehouse. They've turned off the internet so you'll need to give out hard copies of the new safety information.
JOHN	Alex? What are you /
ALEX	I didn't know where else to go. I walked back to the house but Mum wasn't in and the door was locked – so I came here.
JOHN	Come in. Come in. I thought you were... I thought... your feet. They're bleeding. Where are your shoes?
ALEX	They ripped them off my feet.
	Pause.
JOHN	Who did? Why did they?
SI	Let people know it's best to report rather than be reported... about any strays. My neighbour was keeping three pet parakeets and he had an 'accident' while they were confiscating his birds. He has his jaw wired shut now. Stupid bastard. No need to look so worried.
LISA	Oh. No. I've never liked animals anyway – too much... saliva.
ALEX	I ran. I just ran.

Through the police. Through the... I slipped past them all and as I ran I could hear people scream and I just... kept running. I didn't even turn around to look...

I thought I was braver, I thought I could handle it. But...

JOHN   You mustn't /

ALEX   I thought I could help.

         I should have stayed, I should have fought. I
         should have…

LISA   It's a good thing we're doing isn't it? Making it
         safer.

SI   Sure.

         It will be like the whole thing never happened in
         a few weeks. It's a pity about the parks and the
         pets… but it's for the greater good.

JOHN   Oh, my darling. Do you want me to get your
         mother /

ALEX   No! No. Please. Just let me…

JOHN   I'll make you up a room. I'll get bandages for
         your feet.

ALEX   Please don't… please don't get her.

         LISA *coughs.*

SI   Could you cover your mouth please. They said it's
         airborne now.

LISA   Did they? How do you know that?

SI   Can you stop it. Lisa. Stop it with the questions.
         I'm in charge here. Not every statement I make
         needs to be followed up with a series of questions.
         I'm tired of being questioned. Could it be that I'm
         simply doing the right thing, that I simply know
         what I'm doing.

         Just take my fucking statement as fact.

LISA   Of course. I'm sorry /

SI   I've had enough of your questions today.

         Pause.

JOHN   I haven't seen your mother today. But I'll go around in the morning and explain, okay?

ALEX   What they're doing, John. They're burning everything. This isn't about saving anything. It's about destroying everything that's in the way.

A scene with no dialogue.

We see NANCY *lay sewing pins out one by one, side by side.*

She then pours herself a glass of wine – she enjoys a sip.

We see her pick up one pin. She studies it and then drops it in her wine glass.

She continues to drop pins into her glass of wine.

Frame.

> *Focus.*
>
> *Fuck up.*
>
> *Foxes.*
>
> *Fix.*
>
> *These.*
>
> *I can't stop.*
>
> *I won't stop.*

Frame.

> *Focus.*
>
> *Fuck up.*
>
> *Foxes.*
>
> *Fix.*
>
> *These.*
>
> *I can't stop.*
>
> *I won't stop.*

Frame.

> *Focus.*
>
> *Fuck up.*
>
> *Foxes.*
>
> *Fix.*
>
> *These.*
>
> *I can't stop.*
>
> *I won't stop.*

NANCY   I don't want her visiting me.

JOHN   She's your daughter. She'll want to speak to you.

NANCY   After her father… she gets so upset with hospitals… not that you can really call this a hospital any more… They said I was lucky to even get a bed.

           Please, ask her not to come. I just need a little time. I just need a little more… Was she scared?

JOHN   I think it's fair to say Alex's feathers had been ruffled. It didn't sound good, what she saw… what she /

NANCY   Will you tell her I love her? Just tell her… I'll be home when I feel better.

           Silence.

JOHN   I'm sorry.

NANCY   Why?

JOHN   I never knew it was so bad.

NANCY   It's fine. I didn't die. I didn't even want to. I just… you know.

           Time passes.

JOHN   Like that polar bear?

NANCY   What?

JOHN   That polar bear in that zoo that hits its head off the ground. There was something on the radio about it last year. Shouldn't have been so out of its natural habitat or something.

NANCY   I'd like to go to Alaska.

JOHN   I imagine it's beautiful.

NANCY   Promise me we can go.

JOHN   Promise.

Time passes.

Why pins, Nancy? Why of all things did you
swallow pins?

Silence.

NANCY   I had a hunger for something more. That's all.

JOHN   It could have killed you.

NANCY   It could have done many things but it didn't. The
doctors said the body, particularly the mouth can
handle more than we can imagine.

Time passes.

You can go home now, my dearest. You deserve
some rest.

Make sure you wrap up next time won't you? It
gets cold at night now without the street lamps.
You can't go around without a jacket. Wear that
nice navy one I got you for your birthday. You
look so handsome in it.

JOHN   Thank you.

NANCY   You shouldn't look so sad – it's a compliment.
You suit navy.

JOHN   No it's just…

NANCY   What?

What is it?

Is it something with Alex?

JOHN   No. No.

NANCY   If it's the navy jacket, it's easy to replace I know
how clumsy you are with /

JOHN   They burnt down my home. I went back this
morning – and it was just gone.

They caught three sparrows resting on my roof.

They said it was for the greater good.

I thought if I stayed still that all of this – all of whatever is happening would just pass me by… what a fool.

NANCY   Oh. John.

JOHN   Your house is fine. I thought I'd stay there with Alex. I'll get that red-wine stain out of the carpet in the living room for you. Just elbow grease needed, really.

NANCY   I'm so /

JOHN   It's a lot, isn't it. All of this.

They've started shooting all the animals in the zoo too. Anything with four legs or two wings they're killing. As a precaution.

Silence.

I thought it was meant to get less frightening as you got older.

JAMIE   Please don't go.

LISA   You've done nothing to /

JAMIE   I built that /

LISA   Stalemate.

       You know if you drop this. If you drop all of this,
       I'll stay. If you can just go back to what you
       were... I'll stay because I still love you.

       But I want to be with you, just you.

JAMIE   Please don't go. I need you. I don't know what I'll
       do without you.

       But I can't... It's desperate. Why can't you see...
       it's desperate out there.

       Silence.

LISA   I've left forty quid on the counter. In case you
       need it.

       Okay?

SI	They've called out the police.
JOHN	Have they.
SI	Because she is still missing…
JOHN	Who is missing?
SI	That lion. From the zoo. They managed to shoot everything else but she got away. Bad planning if you ask me. Bad fucking planning. I like that thought though, of that lion just roaming free, in amongst the streets. When I first started thinking about it I got hard. Hard for the first time in six months /
JOHN	Oh, shut up.

Silence.

SI	That's not nice, John. No need for that.
JOHN	I'm afraid I don't have much patience for small talk.
SI	Good news though, I think the football will /

JOHN grabs **SI** *by the collar. As if he might kiss him, as if he might throw him.*

Silence.

JOHN	How dare you. How dare you make small talk while everything else falls apart. You lucky fuck.
	You lucky fuck for not seeing it. For not seeing what is there. What is out there.

JOHN *lets go.*

SI	The world isn't falling apart, it's getting better. It's natural selection at its most /
JOHN	You've no idea.
SI	No. That's the thing. I do. I see everything so clearly it would frighten you.

JAMIE This.

    JAMIE *gestures to the outside.*

    This is what we will lose. Look out the window, this is what we will lose.

    It's beautiful, Lisa. It's beautiful and we'll lose it. It will all die under our watch.

    And I want to make sure that isn't so.

LISA And I want normal. Just normal, nothing more. I'd never had normal before you – never had it. And I know that my life won't save the world, my life won't be filled with any great gestures but I think that's okay. Because this was enough for me. You were enough for me. But I am clearly not enough for you.

JAMIE I love you, Lisa. I love you so much I ache but this is bigger than us. It's bigger than two people trying to /

LISA But what if it isn't. What if in two weeks' time everything just goes back to normal and /

JAMIE Fuck's sake. Why can't you see. It's gone too far now.

    We can't just sit by and hope it just goes back to what we had – and what had before was fucked as well. We've just gotten used to that.

    We need to change. We need to wake up. My life and your life and the life of everyone around us is at stake.

    Because they're destroying everything and you're buying popcorn for the show.

    So. Help me.

    I'm finding a new way. A better way. Simpler, stronger, local and less.

LISA	Everything is sick now, Jamie. Everything is ill and dying. All the animals /
JAMIE	The animals are fine, Lisa. In the shed I've got healthy foxes and in the wheelie bin – hedgehogs and shrews and in eaves of the attic – pigeons, sparrows and magpies. I've got healthy animals.

I'm trying to breed those birds. I'll release them when all of this has passed.

It's their world too.

Silence.

SI	My daughter will be so proud of me.
JOHN	I hope she would know better than that.
LISA	How do you know you're not infected? Maybe I'm infected.
JAMIE	The only thing you are infected with is fear. Fear is poisonous and contagious. They are scaring you so you stay in your place, so you burn and eat and kill and don't notice it because it pacifies you. Because you're scared to ask – why?

And being compliant might taste good but it fucking rots your insides.

I'm building a new world in our garden.

LISA	But what if I can't be a part of it.
JAMIE	If you stay, I can help you save yourself.

So. Stay.

They turned off the gas
They've stopped the ambulances
There is no money left to pay the doctors
               There is nowhere left to put the dead

          The trees are
               The birds are
                    The streets are
                         The rivers
                              The oceans
                                   The icebergs

Something about icebergs
It's too hot

                              And it's too cold
                              And it's big.

          It's bigger than words what's happening.
               Bigger than words.

JAMIE   Can I help you?

SI   I'm looking for Lisa.

JAMIE   I'm Jamie. Her boyfriend.

SI   Oh. I didn't know she /

JAMIE   Didn't you?

Silence.

SI   Do you know where I might /

JAMIE   So you're the boss? The big guy. The main… man.

SI   Something like that. It's a pity I missed her, I must dash /

JAMIE   What do you do with the bodies of the animals you kill? Consider it an unofficial enquiry.

SI   We do as we're told – we burn them.

JAMIE   Like how they used to gas and burn people?

SI   Do you know where Lisa is?

JAMIE   No.

The sound of a bird chirping.

SI   What was that?

JAMIE   Better go, you'll be late for work.

The sound of the bird chirping again.

SI   Have you got /

JAMIE   No.

SI   If you have – it's dangerous – you're endangering yourself.

Silence.

JAMIE   Something might have flown in from the garden.

SI   Might it have?

JAMIE   I'm not scared of you.

            It's just hysteria.

SI   Oh yeah? Must have been a lot of hysteria then.

JAMIE   If you ask me I think they're seeing what they can
            get away with. Testing our limits. First they kill the
            birds, then the foxes and next it will be us. They'll
            kill the poor first when we run out of food. They'll
            kill the poor for the rest of us to eat. After all people
            just love to eat meat... And no one will notice or
            care, just like no one cared about the birds.

SI   Best report those birds.

            Or I'll do it for you.

            Oh and be careful, they didn't find that lion that
            escaped from the zoo and it will be hungry.
            Hungry for those birds.

ALEX   I would have come and got you.

NANCY   John walked me home, well, pushed me. He said I
            needed a wheelchair, which is ridiculous. It's not
            my feet that are sore. The hospital has run out
            painkillers, so they gave me a box of miniatures.
            I've never really liked Midori.

ALEX   You were hurt?

NANCY   I was overwhelmed.

ALEX   By me?

NANCY   Maybe.

ALEX   You didn't want to see me?

NANCY   No, I didn't want you to see me. I didn't want to
            scare you.

ALEX   I wouldn't have been scared. I wanted to see you.

NANCY   I am sorry.

ALEX   For what?

            Silence.

NANCY   John said they chased you away? From the park.
            I'm sorry. I'm sorry it didn't work out the way you
            wanted it to.

ALEX   It wasn't what I expected.

NANCY   I tell you what, Alex, when I go, you can put that
            on my tombstone. In the hardest granite you can
            find, under my name you can carve the words – 'It
            wasn't what I expected'.

            Some in the hospital said they're going to go and
            kill that dolphin. The one up near where Grandma
            used to live. Euthanasia – it swam into the glass
            and split its skull.

            Silence.

ALEX   It didn't work, the protest. It didn't... I really
       thought it would do something but it just... I don't
       know how you fix something this big.

       I don't where I... or how we... it didn't feel
       naive... It didn't...

       Silence.

       It's creeping out of this postcode, whatever it is,
       whatever all of this is, it's creeping out.

NANCY Or maybe it was always there.

       Funny that it's a pity when a dolphin is to be killed
       but not when it's a fox.

       We should go and look for the cat.

ALEX   I thought you were scared to go out?

JOHN   How much would I have to pay you to sleep
       with me?

NANCY I'm not sure what to be scared of any more.

SI   Excuse me?

NANCY Rumour has it that there was a lion strolling
       around the garden centre last week.

JOHN   How much would I have to pay you to sleep
       with me?

SI   I didn't think I'd be your type.

JOHN   You're not.

       But if the world is going to hell I refuse to... Well.
       I'd like to have a little fun.

SI   And I'm your best bet?

JOHN   Considering my limited access to... other parts of
       the city.

       Yes.

       I've got money. I'll pay whatever you want.

SI	What is it you want to do?
JOHN	I want to hit you. I want to beat you until you bleed. I want to use my belt. I want to cause big welts on your back. I want you to beg me to stop. And I want you to hit me. Square in the jaw. Don't look so surprised.
SI	No it just… sounds animal.
JOHN	What I'm proposing is strictly human.
SI	You always struck me as the tender type.
JOHN	Take a look outside. I've started sleeping with a kitchen knife under my pillow.
SI	People are beginning to revolt.
JAMIE	Why are you back here? You told them I was here!
JOHN	So. Do you want to do this or not?
LISA	What is that smell?
JOHN	Name a number.
JAMIE	A fox bit my hand. Tore at it. While I was sleeping. It's got infected now. That's what smells. Gone septic /
LISA	I'm calling a doctor!
JAMIE	Why would you? You did this.
LISA	No I didn't.
JAMIE	They came around with guns and with gas and they tore holes in the roof and through the plaster and kicked our doors in. But you know what – fuck you, Lisa. I let them go. I let all the animals go before they got here.

At least twenty foxes, fifteen pigeons and six squirrels. Back out there. If I did one small thing, I saved them – for now. For now, they are free. I'd forgotten what it felt like – to be free.

Silence.

LISA   I came back to check on you, Jamie. I was worried, I was /

JAMIE   That man. That man from your work, the man with blood on his hands and teeth and his money.

LISA   Maybe, Jamie. Maybe it was him. But it wasn't me. I was coming back to /

JAMIE   They beat me.

Once they realised I let the animals go.

They hit me until I blacked out.

I think they thought I was dead.

But fuck them.

LISA   Please let me /

JAMIE   This is only the beginning.

LISA   I'm sorry, Jamie, I'm so sorry.

JAMIE   No, I'm sorry for you. You were never brave enough to see what was happening. You were never strong enough to resist. You are scared and weak. Your energy was put into all the wrong things. I feel sorry for you. Because when it changes – because it has to, it must, you'll be lost.

LISA   You don't know what you're saying, you're confused.

JAMIE   No. I'm not.

LISA   It's still wild. They're still wild. You've got to look after yourself. We both have.

JAMIE   People are turning on each other.

          It's not the animals drawing blood, it's people against people now.

          There are no civilians in this war. Not any more.

          Is that blood on your /

LISA   Please can I /

JAMIE   Why didn't you believe me?

          Why didn't you believe me from the start?

You

    They

        They beat her

            They just

                Why are you

                    I'm not

                        Who can

JOHN	Have you been crying, my dear?
ALEX	It's just…
	Silence.
JOHN	Do you want me to leave?
ALEX	No. Please don't.

Burning all the

    Every single

        Forced to

            So I just

                I don't understand

                    It's not

                      It's not.

JAMIE	How couldn't you see? How couldn't you see it was so bad?
LISA	I thought…

JAMIE   You don't belong here.

LISA   But I thought...

JAMIE   Before you go. I want you to have something.

             And there was blood. Everywhere.

             I felt like being sick.

             But I thought

             But I thought

             I thought

             I thought

LISA   Why were you at my house?

             I thought

SI   Why haven't you been at work?

             I thought

LISA   How dare you /

SI   Lisa, I /

LISA   Why were you at my house?

SI   Your boyfriend. He's unusual.

LISA   You piece of shit. You reported him.

SI   You know it's dangerous to keep animals. No
             matter how well intended. I had no choice.

LISA   They destroyed my home. Do you know how long
             it took me to... And they don't really know
             anything about it. They have no fucking clue
             what's happening.

SI   They know enough to know it's dangerous.

LISA   But /

SI   You didn't seem to care much about it until it
             destroyed your home.

LISA   You sleazy self-serving /

SI   Well. That's not very nice.

LISA   You've taken everything from me.

SI   I don't do what I do for no reason, Lisa. I'm not…
              I have a daughter and let me tell you, just about
              any decent father would kill every single fox in
              this city with his bare hands if it meant he got to
              hug his little girl.

LISA   But you've destroyed… I don't even have a home
              to… why is hugging your daughter worth more /

              SI *slaps* **LISA.**

SI   Take a look outside.

              You don't belong here any more.

JOHN   I realise it's not exactly Alaska… but I tried.

NANCY   What did they /

JOHN   Penguins. It was the penguin enclosure. But they
             gassed them all. Much easier to kill birds who
             don't fly.

NANCY   I thought they'd shut up this place weeks ago after
             they killed all the animals.

JOHN   I slipped security his weekly wage. We've got
             twenty minutes. I must admit, it looks a little more
             atmospheric on the leaflet.

NANCY   You're very sweet, John.

             You must save your money to rebuild.

JOHN   No, you can't rebuild. Not really. You can only
             move on.
             It's only bricks and mortar.

             Silence.

             Does your head feel clear?

NANCY   No. But it feels like it might be clearing.

JOHN   You scared me.

NANCY   You brought me here to say that?

JOHN   You scared me. I didn't know how much /

NANCY   Neither did I.

             It's amazing isn't it… all that… ice.

JOHN   Concrete. It's painted concrete, not ice.

NANCY   Feels like the world could end and we wouldn't
             even know about it.

JOHN   If the end of the world was right now, I would be
             glad I'd have your hand to hold. It is the only, and

the best answer I have found to the problem of living. Having something to hold on to if the end should come.

Pause.

NANCY   You're a sentimental cunt.

JOHN   Nancy!

NANCY   I've always wanted to say *that word* out loud and all this talk of the end of the world. Well, if I can't swear in Alaska then where can I?

JOHN   Yes. Well. Quite.

NANCY   If the world ended right now, you know what I'd be most upset about?

JOHN   What?

NANCY   Not trying harder.

JOHN   I think you've tried pretty hard.

NANCY   No. I'm not sure I have.

Times passes.

JOHN   I had a thought, Nancy. I had a very clear thought while trying to fall asleep last night.

JOHN *pulls out a gun.*

NANCY   What is that, John? What's going on?

JOHN   It's alarmingly easy to buy these now. They were practically selling them in the vegetable aisle.

NANCY   What's happening... what are you...

JOHN   I bought this because I thought you could use it, if you wanted to. If you wanted to kill yourself. I was thinking about it. About how impossible life can be. And I can see why you would want to kill yourself. So. I bought this. And I wanted to give it to you with one bullet. Because I know you've found life impossible and I don't want you going on thinking life is impossible. So. Here.

I know how much you wanted to see Alaska. And I thought it would be an incredibly atmospheric place to die.

JOHN *goes to hand* **NANCY** *the gun.*

It is incredibly selfish to force someone to live if they simply want to die.

And I fear it's not going to get any better.

She takes the gun.

LISA   Do you know what time it starts?

ALEX   No idea.

LISA   I thought there would be more people.

ALEX   The crowds are the other side of the park.

LISA   This is the first time I've seen this.

            Why are you here?

ALEX   It's just... important to watch the things that
            scare you.

            Are you watching? Or are you protesting?

LISA   I don't know.

            I thought... I thought... I don't know what I...

ALEX   I did everything I could think of to do... but...
            but... nothing...

LISA   I didn't do anything... Nothing at all.

            LISA *pulls out a perfectly formed egg.*

            Small, beautiful in its own way.

            She passes it to **ALEX.**

            ALEX *holds it carefully in her hands.*

            It could be a sparrow or a magpie or maybe
            a pigeon.

            My boyfriend has been keeping them.

            You've got to keep it somewhere warm.
            Somewhere close to your skin.

ALEX   I thought these were illegal.

LISA   I think we've all lived beyond the law now. I think
            you should have it.

ALEX   What do I do with it?

LISA   You look after it.

                And then you let it go.

                And then most importantly – you just let it be.

                I've given out half a dozen. Hopefully some will make it.

                But you never know… you never really know if what you're doing makes a difference.

                We should have never have touched them.

                Never have touched those animals in the first place.

ALEX   Why aren't you keeping it?

LISA   Because I don't deserve it.

                Silence.

                A rustling sound.

                What's that?

ALEX   What's what?

LISA   There in the bushes.

ALEX   I can't see /

LISA   Don't move.

                The sound of a gunshot.

                Loud.

                Frightening.

                The sound lingers on.

Silence.

NANCY   I don't want to die, John.

It's a stupid compulsion. Living. Pointless really.

But out of simple curiosity, I'd like to see how it all plays out.

But thank you.

My dear friend. Thank you.

She hands him back the gun and he puts it away.

She kisses him on the cheek and holds his hand.

JOHN   It's horrible isn't it. This enclosure.

NANCY   Yes.

Pause.

God bless this mess.

JOHN   Oh, Nancy, God left here a long time ago.

I don't know how

I've no idea how we

Can we even

How can we

And you felt?

You felt.

What?

What did you feel?

And you felt?

You felt.

What?

What did you feel?

And you felt?

And you felt?

And you felt?

Can you even?

Can you

Can you

Can you even

Can you

ALEX   I ran. I ran just like you said.

            I went back an hour later but she was gone.

            They were digging through the soot when I left.
            Looking for bodies of the foxes, they found the
            body of a baby too. An abandoned baby. Under the
            swing set.

            The army pushed us all away after that. What's
            that?

NANCY   A vintage Chanel.

ALEX   Why are you tearing it up?

            NANCY *tears up the dress.*

            Opens a bottle.

            ***And throws it onto the dress. The smell of
            whiskey fills the air.***

NANCY   Do you think this will work?

ALEX   What are you doing with that whiskey?

NANCY   Darling, this is not just a whiskey. It's from 1932
            and it's bloody cask-strength... It was going to be
            my fortieth wedding-anniversary present for your
            father... I think he'd rather have a laugh at me
            throwing it over my Chanel.

ALEX   What are you doing?

NANCY   I'm going to start a fire. Start a fire at one of the
            blockades so I can get out of this fucking city.
            Because I can't stand it any more – I can't just
            stand by. You were right. We're trapped.

            I always had this feeling – just here – just to the
            right of my heart and now I know what that was –
            it's anger. And what I see so clearly now is that
            anger is hope. And I've got to do something with
            it. I've just got to...

And this is the only thing I could think of to do.

To destroy something. To burn it down.

ALEX   No.

There has been enough fucking destruction.

I'm angry too. You know.

I'm fucking furious. I'm so fucking furious it hurts.

Because
We
Deserve
Better.

But this… this isn't the answer.

LISA   How is your hand?

JAMIE   Now the power is back on I tried to cauterise it
with the toaster. It helped. A little. It's still rotting.
Why are you back?

LISA   I saw her, Jamie. I saw her. She was just like you
said. She was just like…

She was incredible. She was in the bushes near to
the park and I was scared because… well, the way
she looked at me. She was… incredible. And I was
so scared and quiet. It was all just really quiet.

And I found this gun, sitting on a bench, just
yesterday and so I took it – I never wanted to use
it, I never wanted to… And it was pressed into the
skin on my hip and then it was in my hand and
then my finger was on the trigger.

The girl next to me just ran, just vanished and it
was just me… me and this lion.

JAMIE   You shot her?

LISA   No.

I didn't.

I looked her in the eyes and I just... I fired into the sky.

SI   Shouldn't you be drinking champagne? Considering the roads are finally opening.

JOHN   How are your profits? Not good for business is it... all this... returning to normal. Although it's a new type of normal now.

SI   Funny how that happened after they burnt the last park. Some of those idiots think it's all still happening. I suppose it will take a while for everyone to calm down.

JOHN   There isn't a scrap of remorse on you. All that damage caused. Animals and houses and hospitals and all that... sickness. It'll take years for them to fix the damage.

SI   My mother used to knit these little dolls of the children who had been born after that nuclear power plant blew up. Kids who were more bones than breath, more scars than skin, more limbs than life. They didn't really take off. She said she'd made them so the rest of us remember to live. Someone has to be pulled apart so the rest of us remember to live. She said that.

JOHN   That's terrifying.

SI   Maybe.

LISA   You're right.

            It's gone too far. It's gone too fucking far.

            And I don't want to know.

            I don't want to know how it gets worse than this.

            LISA *sits next to* **JAMIE.**

            Silence.

JAMIE   You're joining me?

ALEX *pulls out the egg.*

ALEX   It could be a magpie or a sparrow or a /

NANCY   Who gave you it?

ALEX   Just a person. Who saw something.

NANCY   We're responsible for it?

ALEX   We always were.

         Silence.

NANCY   I don't where to put all of this… how I… what
         I've…

ALEX   I know.

         I know.

         But we have to do something about it…

         It's a different way of life now. We need a
         different way of life.

SI   You know they're closing this pub? Someone
         bought it. Wants to knock it down, build some
         flats for all the folk whose houses got torched. I
         hope philanthropy isn't contagious… that's a joke.

JOHN   I hate this pub. I always have done.

SI   Then why did you come?

JOHN   I suppose habit has a funny way of stopping you
         questioning things.

SI   Want me to buy you one for the road?

JOHN   No. I think I've had enough.

SI   Would you like to meet my daughter? Daisy. She
         is just playing outside.

         Her mother isn't very well… she had an accident.
         So Daisy will be living with me full time.

JOHN   Does it always work out well for you?

JAMIE	The foxes will come soon. They get hungry at night.
LISA	Does it hurt? When they eat you?
JAMIE	No more or less than anything else.
	If you roll up your sleeves they can get a better bite.
LISA	…Okay.

LISA *rolls up her sleeves.*

You know in a parallel universe we are parents.

JAMIE	I know.
LISA	You'd have been a good dad.
JAMIE	Yeah?
LISA	Yeah.
JOHN	Make sure you get her that guinea pig – won't you?
	Because one day, one day she'll see who you really are.
SI	Are you sure I can't buy you a drink?
JOHN	Goodbyes are always so underwhelming when they happen.
	Aren't they?
NANCY	I forgot…
ALEX	What?
NANCY	I forgot to say – the cat. I found him on the doormat. He'd been hit, or beaten or… but he came home to die. I'm sorry. I know we've both had quite enough of death.
	I thought I'd replant those roses. Under the window in the kitchen and we could bury him there. They were your father's favourite flower and the bees love them.
ALEX	I can't remember the last time I saw a bee.

LISA   Can I just kiss you? Really soft. Just here… and
            here… and here…

            You going to kiss me back then?

JAMIE   Sure. Sure I'll kiss you back. Just here… and
            here… and here…

LISA   That's nice.

JAMIE   So that lion is still out there?

LISA   I hope so.

            They wait. Time passes.

JAMIE   I'm glad you're here.

            You deserve this.

When they ask us what we saw and what we did

All of us will just say

I stood and watched

> *I stood and watched*

> > *I stood and watched*

And she was just standing there

Above us all.

Looking right through us all.

Calm, you'd describe her as calm.

As she tied that knot around her neck

Someone gasped

Another person just burst into tears

But no one said, anything

> *Nothing at all.*

And she stepped off

Just like that.

Swinging and struggling from the tree branch

Hanging right there in the middle of Sloane Square

Hands by her side

Gasping for air

Twitching and twisting.

Not saying a word

> *Nothing at all.*

And then the pigeons landed one by one on her body.

Pigeon on top of pigeon.

Coming from nowhere

        Coming from everywhere

Perching on her skin

And then they began to eat her flesh

*Began to tear at her clothes and her skin and her
hair and her nails*

And her body just swung side to side

Hundreds of pigeons.

Beaks scratching at her

        Picking her apart

           With feathers falling through the air

Black and blue and green fell from the sky.

Blood tipped and torn

And the noise of the flesh tearing

The sound of bones being ripped from muscle

Eating the bones and the bile and blood

Wings fluttering on top of one another

And as the body began to disappear

Their beaks turned into noses

And their wings into arms

Their feathers flatten and dulled into skin

Squawks became shouts

Eyes shifted to the front of their head

And they grew teeth

        And tumours

           And toes

And their bodies became wrapped in cloth

And they wiped the blood off their faces and topped up their Oyster cards

And took the District Line into town

And no one noticed.

No one turned and stopped and said

> *Not this way.*
>
> *Not now.*
>
> *Not this way.*
>
> *Not now.*
>
> *Not this way.*
>
> *Not now.*

What was left of her dripped onto the ground.

The grass will grow back the colour of blood

A new life will begin again

Entirely indifferent to what came before.

And the rope was just left hanging, swinging

They'll take it down before Christmas

It will get in the way of all the lights.

The End.

Other Titles in this Series

A Nick Hern Book

Human Animals first published as a paperback original in Great Britain in 2016
by Nick Hern Books Limited, The Glasshouse, 49a Goldhawk Road, London
W12 8QP, in association with the Royal Court Theatre, London

Human Animals copyright © 2016 Stef Smith

Stef Smith has asserted her right to be identified as the author of this work

Front cover image: Lovers

Designed and typeset by Nick Hern Books, London
Printed and bound in Great Britain by CPI Group (UK) Ltd

A CIP catalogue record for this book is available from the British Library

ISBN 978 1 84842 528 6

www.nickhernbooks.co.uk

facebook.com/nickhernbooks

twitter.com/nickhernbooks